Put Beginning Readers on the Right Track with
ALL ABOARD READING™

The All Aboard Reading series is especially designed for beginning readers. Written by noted authors and illustrated in full color, these are books that children really want to read—books to excite their imagination, expand their interests, make them laugh, and support their feelings. With fiction and nonfiction stories that are high interest and curriculum-related, All Aboard Reading books offer something for every young reader. And with four different reading levels, the All Aboard Reading series lets you choose which books are most appropriate for your children and their growing abilities.

Picture Readers
Picture Readers have super-simple texts, with many nouns appearing as rebus pictures. At the end of each book are 24 flash cards—on one side is a rebus picture; on the other side is the written-out word.

Station Stop 1
Station Stop 1 books are best for children who have just begun to read. Simple words and big type make these early reading experiences more comfortable. Picture clues help children to figure out the words on the page. Lots of repetition throughout the text helps children to predict the next word or phrase—an essential step in developing word recognition.

Station Stop 2
Station Stop 2 books are written specifically for children who are reading with help. Short sentences make it easier for early readers to understand what they are reading. Simple plots and simple dialogue help children with reading comprehension.

Station Stop 3
Station Stop 3 books are perfect for children who are reading alone. With longer text and harder words, these books appeal to children who have mastered basic reading skills. More complex stories captivate children who are ready for more challenging books.

In addition to All Aboard Reading books, look for All Aboard Math Readers™ (fiction stories that teach math concepts children are learning in school); All Aboard Science Readers™ (nonfiction books that explore the most fascinating science topics in age-appropriate language); All Aboard Poetry Readers™ (funny, rhyming poems for readers of all levels); and All Aboard Mystery Readers™ (puzzling tales where children piece together evidence with the characters).

All Aboard for happy reading!

To Moms Group and The Bells, for
helping me to keep from bugging out
about parenthood—G.L.C.

I have spent many enjoyable hours from
childhood on watching insects—P.M.

GROSSET & DUNLAP
Published by the Penguin Group
Penguin Group (USA) Inc., 375 Hudson Street, New York, New York 10014, U.S.A.
Penguin Group (Canada), 90 Eglinton Avenue East, Suite 700,
Toronto, Ontario, Canada M4P 2Y3 (a division of Pearson Penguin Canada Inc.)
Penguin Books Ltd, 80 Strand, London WC2R 0RL, England
Penguin Ireland, 25 St Stephen's Green, Dublin 2, Ireland
(a division of Penguin Books Ltd)
Penguin Group (Australia), 250 Camberwell Road, Camberwell, Victoria 3124, Australia
(a division of Pearson Australia Group Pty Ltd)
Penguin Books India Pvt Ltd, 11 Community Centre, Panchsheel Park,
New Delhi - 110 017, India
Penguin Group (NZ), 67 Apollo Drive, Mairangi Bay, Auckland 1311, New Zealand
(a division of Pearson New Zealand Ltd)
Penguin Books (South Africa) (Pty) Ltd, 24 Sturdee Avenue, Rosebank,
Johannesburg 2196, South Africa

Penguin Books Ltd, Registered Offices:
80 Strand, London WC2R 0RL, England

Text copyright © 2007 by Ginjer L. Clarke. Illustrations copyright © 2007 by Pete Mueller. All
rights reserved. Published by Grosset & Dunlap, a division of Penguin Young Readers Group,
345 Hudson Street, New York, New York 10014. ALL ABOARD SCIENCE READER and
GROSSET & DUNLAP are trademarks of Penguin Group (USA) Inc. Printed in the U.S.A.

ISBN 978-0-448-44543-4   10 9 8 7 6 5 4 3 2 1

BUG OUT!

The World's Creepiest, Crawliest Critters

By Ginjer L. Clarke
Illustrated by Pete Mueller

Grosset & Dunlap

Introduction
A Bit About Bugs

Do you like bugs?

Bugs can be really creepy,

but they can also be really cool.

One bug stabs its prey

and sucks it dry.

Another bug plucks its prey

out of the air.

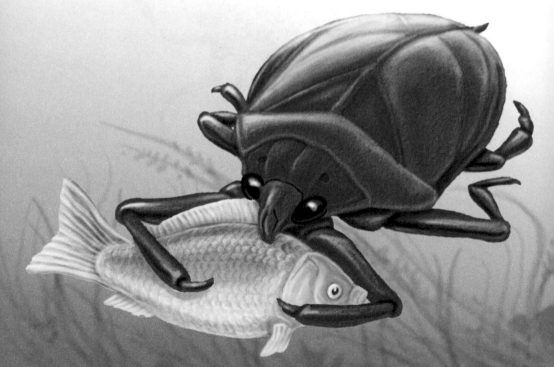

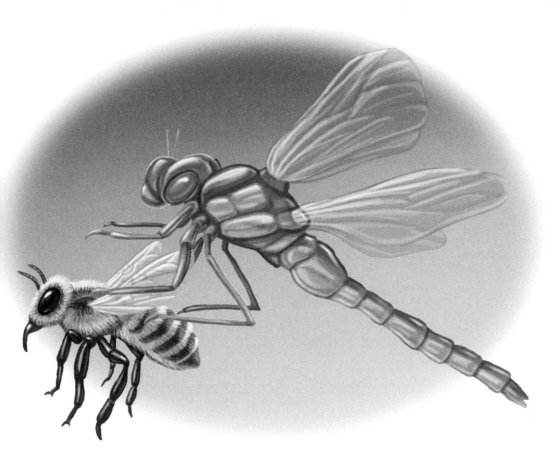

There are more bugs in the world

than any other type of animal.

Some bugs can hurt you.

Other bugs help plants grow.

Some bugs hunt for their prey.

Other bugs stay hidden away.

Let's uncover more about bugs!

Are all bugs insects?

No.

Insects have six legs, antennae, and three parts to their bodies. This long-horned beetle has a head, thorax, and abdomen. It is an insect.

Most insects also have wings.

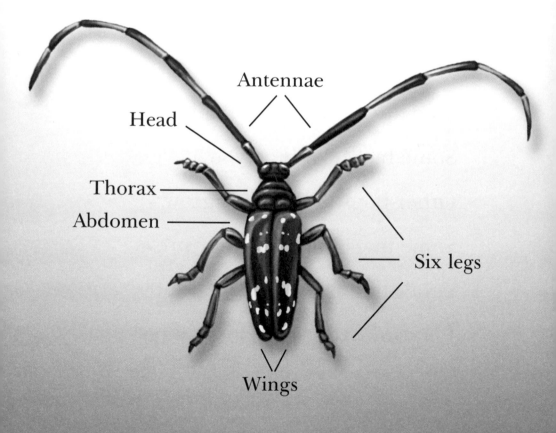

Antennae

Head

Thorax

Abdomen

Six legs

Wings

Abdomen

Eight legs

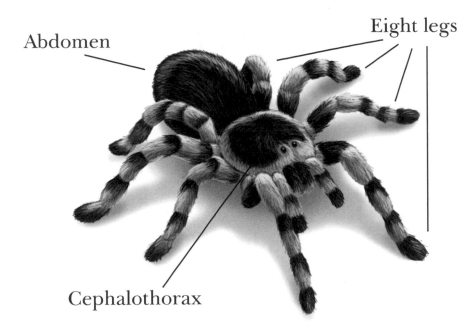

Cephalothorax

This tarantula has eight legs
and only two body parts.
Spiders are called bugs,
but they are not insects.
They are arachnids
(say: uh-RAK-nidz).
Scorpions are arachnids, too.
There are more than 70,000
kinds of arachnids.

Chapter 1
Bugs That Hurt

The **tarantula hawk wasp**
lives in the deserts
of North and South America.
This insect kills tarantulas!
A tarantula is often bigger than
a tarantula hawk wasp, but the wasp
has a special way of attacking.

This tarantula hawk wasp swoops in

and stings a tarantula.

The tarantula is not dead,

but it cannot move.

The wasp drags the spider

to a tunnel in the desert.

It lays an egg on the spider's belly.

For the next month or so,

the wasp does this to

20 or more spiders.

After the eggs hatch,

each baby wasp eats a tarantula.

Whip

Hairy

Sand

African

Scorpions have eight legs and

two big front claws

called pincers (say: PIN-serz).

Scorpions also have powerful stingers

on the end of their tails.

They use their stingers to kill prey

and fight enemies.

There are more than

1,300 types of scorpions.

Most scorpions live in warm places

like deserts and jungles.

Pow!

This **black fat-tailed scorpion**

curls its stinger over its head

and jabs a grasshopper.

The poison in the scorpion's stinger

kills the grasshopper.

This poison is so powerful,

it can even kill humans.

If you ever see a scorpion,

do not touch it!

The **giant water bug**

is poisonous, too.

Its poison usually does not

harm people, but its bite hurts.

The giant water bug eats insects,

fish, and small frogs and snakes.

It lives in ponds and streams

in many places all over the world.

It can grow up to four inches long.

That's about the size of your hand.

1   2   3   4

This giant water bug grabs a frog

with its large front pincers.

The water bug stabs the frog

with its sharp beak.

Its poison turns the frog's

insides into mush.

Slurp!

The water bug uses its beak to

drink the frog's blood and guts.

Only the frog's empty skin is left over.

One bee sting hurts.

But what if you got stung

by lots of bees?

Ouch!

Killer bees live in warm areas of

North and South America.

They look just like honeybees,

but they attack in huge groups.

A few people have even died when

they were stung many times.

If you see killer bees,

run fast and get inside.

This bear is stealing honey

from a nest of killer bees.

Bzzzzz!

The bees attack quickly.

They chase the bear and sting it.

Bees can sting only once,

and then they die.

The bear runs away.

He will be okay, but he will not

touch that hive again!

What kind of bug sucks blood?

A **mosquito** (say: muh-SKEE-toe).

Mosquitoes live in warm places near water.

Only female mosquitoes drink blood.

Male mosquitoes drink a sweet liquid

from flowers called nectar.

This mosquito bites a cow with

its needle-sharp mouthpart.

It uses a long tube like a straw

to suck up blood.

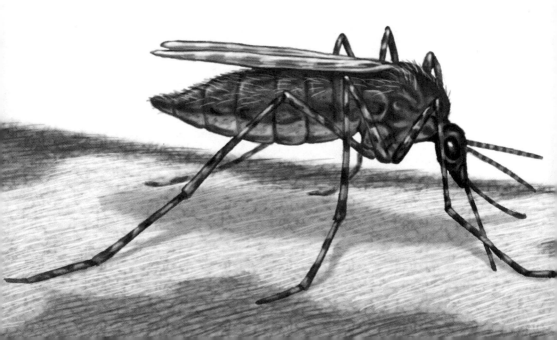

Some mosquitoes bite humans
and drink a little bit of blood.
Their bite does not hurt much,
but it sure is itchy.
Mosquitoes also spread diseases
that can kill people.
If you wear bug spray outside,
the mosquitoes will stay away.
But watch out for these
nasty little bugs!

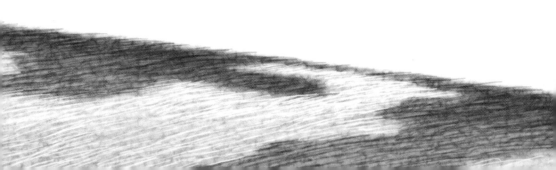

Chapter 2
Bugs That Help

What spider helps in the garden?

A **wolf spider.**

There are 2,000 kinds of

wolf spiders all over the world.

All of them eat insects

that can destroy plants,

like aphids (say: A-fidz),

gypsy moths, and cottonworms.

Chomp!

This wolf spider grabs
a cottonworm and eats it alive.
Wolf spiders live mostly in
forests and gardens, not in houses.
They do not bite people,
but they sure look creepy!

Robber flies also help people.

They eat stinging insects.

Most animals leave bees and wasps

alone, so they do not get stung.

But some robber flies look

a lot like bees and wasps.

This helps them blend in and

keep from being stung or eaten.

This robber fly flies fast next to a wasp.
The wasp does not fly away because
the robber fly looks like a wasp.
Suddenly, the robber fly catches
the wasp with its legs.
The fly goes back to the tree
and drinks the wasp's insides.

Have you ever felt smooth, shiny silk?
People use silk to make clothes,
scarves, sheets, and other things.
Silk is made by **silk moth** caterpillars.
Silk moths do not live in the wild.
They live on silk farms worldwide.
People have used them to make silk
for almost 5,000 years.
Now the moths are too big to fly.

This silk moth caterpillar

covers itself in lots of silk.

It grows the silk inside its body.

It wraps itself in a cocoon

made of one long string of silk.

When the caterpillar comes out of

the cocoon, it will be a moth.

Honeybees make honey.

They also help plants to grow.

Honeybees drink nectar from flowers.

They turn the nectar into honey.

Yum!

Some honeybees live in the wild.

Other honeybees are kept

in hives by people.

People gather the honey from the hives.

We also make things like candles

from the wax inside the hives.

Wild honeybees live in large groups.

They make nests in hollow trees.

Each group has one large queen bee

and thousands of worker bees.

These worker bees are bringing

food to the queen.

They protect the queen and her eggs.

Worker bees also take care of

the baby bees and fix the nest.

They will sting an animal or a person

if it disturbs the nest.

Ladybugs are easy to spot
because of their polka dots.
They live everywhere,
and they eat lots of aphids.
Aphids kill plants and vegetables
that people like to eat.
Without ladybugs, there would be
less good food for us.

Ladybugs are brightly colored.

They can be red, black, yellow, or orange.

These colors warn birds to keep away.

When a bird comes too close,

this ladybug oozes smelly liquid

from its legs to scare off the bird.

If the bird still sticks around,

the ladybug opens its hidden wings

and flies away quickly.

See you later, little ladybug!

Chapter 3
Bugs That Hunt

There are more than 4,000
kinds of **jumping spiders**.
They live all around the world.
They can see very well because
they have four big eyes.
Jumping spiders hunt in the daytime,
mostly in warm, sunny places.
They hide in small cracks
in bad weather and in the winter.

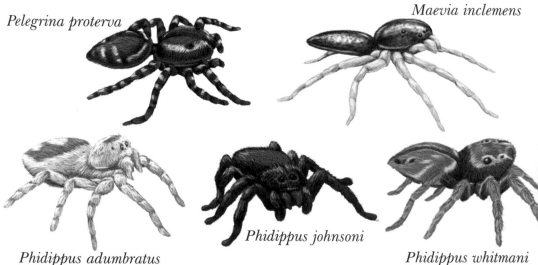

Pelegrina proterva

Maevia inclemens

Phidippus adumbratus

Phidippus johnsoni

Phidippus whitmani

This jumping spider is a sneaky hunter.

It does not spin a web

like other spiders.

It spots a cricket on a leaf.

It jumps from a nearby tree

and lands on the cricket.

The spider kills the cricket

with its big, furry fangs.

Pselliopus sp

Apiomerus crassipes

Zelus bilobus

Leptoglossus occidentalis

The word "assassin"

(say: uh-SAH-sen)

means "one who kills."

There are more than 5,000 kinds of

assassin bugs worldwide.

Some steal prey from spiderwebs.

Others chase their prey.

Most assassin bugs hunt like tigers.

They sneak up slowly

and then pounce on their prey.

This assassin bug grabs a
cockroach with its long legs.
It stabs the roach with
its sharp beak and poisons it.
The roach's insides turn into
a kind of liquid soup.
The assassin bug sucks out the soup
until the roach is empty.
Yuck!

Diving beetles live in ponds
and streams everywhere.
They do not wait until they
are grown-up to hunt.
Both baby and adult beetles
can dive for food.
They eat small fish,
tadpoles, and other beetles.
The adults swim by using their
back legs like oars.

These diving beetles can stay
underwater for a long time.
The adult breathes by storing air
under its wings while it swims.
The baby beetle hangs upside down
and breathes through its tail.
Snap!
Both beetles grab prey
with their sharp jaws.

A baby **dragonfly** lives underwater, too.

It swims for a few months or

sometimes years until it grows up.

Then it becomes a fast flyer

high above the water.

Dragonflies are good hunters.

They have the largest eyes of all insects.

They can see in front, below,

and behind them at the same time.

They can pluck prey out of the air

while they are flying.

Zoom!

This dragonfly zips through
a group of flies.
It snatches up a meal and
keeps on flying.
Now that is fast food!

Army ants are fast, too.

But they live on the ground.

And they have tiny eyes that cannot

see well, so they hunt by smell.

Army ants live in forests

all over the world.

They have lots of workers and

one queen, just like honeybees.

Army ants can bite people.

They will not hurt you

if you stay out of their way.

Thousands of army ants
march in a long line.
They will eat almost anything
in their path, including animals
much bigger than they are.
These ants swarm on a small snake.
They bite the snake many times
until it is dead.
They use their huge jaws to
pull the snake into tiny pieces.
The army ants won this battle!

Chapter 4
Bugs That Hide

Crab spiders come in many colors.

They can change their color

to match different flowers.

This is called camouflage

(say: KAH-muh-flazh).

Some crab spiders live on

only one flower for most of their lives.

They hide in the center of the flower

and wait for prey to come to them.

This crab spider opens its front legs
and waits quietly on a flower.
When a bee buzzes by, the spider
closes its legs and traps the bee.
The crab spider poisons the bee
with its fangs and sucks out
the bee's insides.
The spider tosses the bee away.
Then it sits and waits for more food.

What does a baby doodlebug do?

It digs in the sand and makes

trails that look like doodles.

A doodlebug is also called an **ant lion**

because it eats lots of ants.

But only the baby ant lion digs

in the sand and catches ants.

When it grows up, it will be a

flying insect that looks like a dragonfly.

Ant lions live in sandy areas

all around the world.

This baby ant lion digs a pit.

It hides at the bottom and waits

until an ant falls in.

If the ant tries to climb out,

the ant lion throws sand at it.

Then the ant slides to the bottom.

The ant lion grabs the ant

with its big jaws.

Gulp!

The ant lion sucks the ant dry.

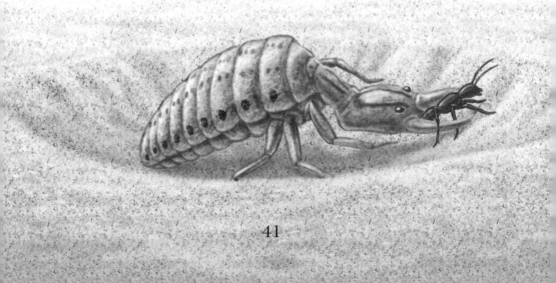

Do you see the bugs on
these thorny branches?
The thorns *are* the bugs!
Thorn bugs come in bright colors
and interesting shapes.
They live mostly in Florida
and South and Central America.

These thorn bugs sit totally still.

They are hiding from birds and lizards

by looking like thorns.

They are also eating tree sap.

Thorn bugs make cuts in tree branches

and drink the sap.

That is the only food they eat.

Hop!

Thorn bugs are also called "treehoppers"

because they jump from tree to tree.

Cicadas (say: sih-KAE-duhz)

live all around the world.

The females lay lots of eggs

in tree branches.

When the babies hatch,

they crawl into the ground.

Some types of cicadas stay

underground for 17 years!

They eat sap from plant and tree roots

and keep growing bigger.

When they are fully grown,

thousands of baby cicadas

come out of the ground

all at the same time.

They shed their shells

and become adults.

The male cicadas sing loudly.

Their songs are so noisy that

sometimes people who are outside

cannot hear each other talking.

When summer is over,

these cicadas die.

But their babies will be back!

The **giant wetapunga** is the

world's heaviest insect.

The largest giant weta ever found

was three times heavier than a mouse!

The giant weta is even

too heavy to jump.

Giant wetas hide all day

in trees and bushes.

They come out at night to

eat berries and small bugs.

They live only on a few

tiny islands in New Zealand.

This giant weta sees a rat

that wants to eat it.

The weta sticks up its spiny back legs

to warn the rat away.

These spines can really hurt

when the giant weta kicks.

The rat scurries off.

And the giant weta goes back

to its hiding spot.

Bugs are everywhere.

They live in trees, underwater,

in the air, on the ground,

and even in houses.

Just look around you,

and have fun bugging out!